Infinite Permission

— *a healing journey home*

poems by Wendy Mulhern

images by Mellissae Lucia

to Edward, who started me on this path
  -Wendy Mulhern

4 Jaymes
and all our
Infinite permission
to be our true
selves.
xxx
M

Introduction

In looking back over these poems, which I wrote over the past year and a half, I am struck by the journey they chronicle — a journey from relative inhibition to great freedom, from constriction to joy, from a dissatisfied sense of myself to a sense of awe — not for what I have made myself to be, but for what I am now freer to reflect; the divine gift of Life. For me, these poems recall luminous moments — of liberation, of compassion, of growth. I'm filled with deep gratitude for having been given so many such moments within this short span of time, and for having been able to capture them.

As I was putting this collection together, I remembered a movie I had recently seen about Mellissae Lucia, an artist who boldly chronicled her journey out of grief through the very art that aided her healing. I resonated with her process, seeing in it the same raw honesty, surrender and receptivity I've found to be entailed in writing poetry. Her beautiful and startling images managed to portray a journey very similar to the one these poems cover. So I asked her to consider a collaboration, and was delighted to find she had been thinking along similar lines.

As we worked to match her images with my poems, an exhilarating synergy set in, along with the joy of finding a kindred spirit in the adventure of art and life.

I hope that, in these poems and images, you'll find joy traveling with us on this exciting ride.

Wendy Mulhern
August, 2012

Contents

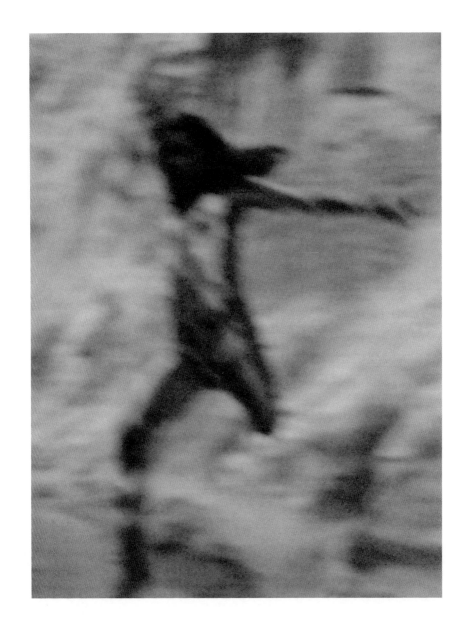

Infinite Permission

The One who made you
never said
Only take a little love
a polite small serving
(being sure to leave plenty
for everyone else)

The One who made you
never said
Just show a little of yourself
not enough so anyone has to notice
(don't be a spectacle)

The One who made you
gives you infinite permission
to take all the love
you possibly can
(for in taking love, you multiply it)

The One who made you
gives you infinite permission
to shine forth everything you are
(for otherwise,
Why would you have been made?)

Birthright

No need to retreat behind your skin
to a small box that thinks without moving
some disconnected separate life within
that dreads a coming time of proving
There is no course of regimented learning
and no certificate required
The potent path of following your yearning
delivers you to where you are inspired
We each are born with full permission
to move in elemental grace
to bring our ancient essence to fruition
to fully fill our pre-established place
Each of us, by right, lives in connection
Our turning, and the world's, bring forth perfection.

Space and Time

You have the right
to take up all the space you take
and you have the right
to take up all the time you need
and you have the right
to be —
to be whatever you are.
There's room for all of you here
and there's room for the time it takes
for you to feel at home
and there's room for you to breathe
and space for your incubation
and time for you to grow.
You are welcome
to everything your soul needs
to be fulfilled.

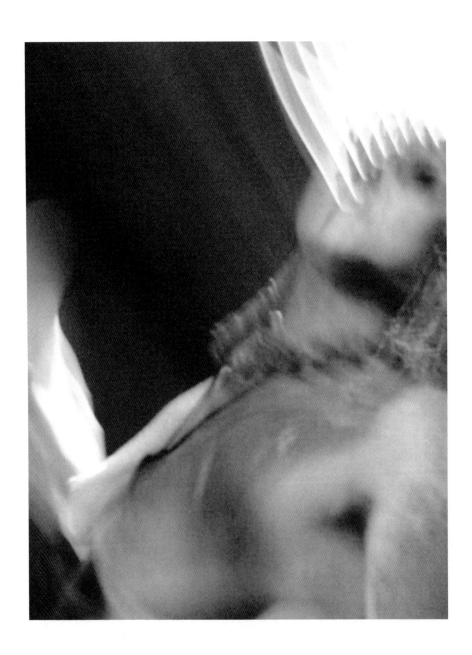

Body and Mind

My body is not
the puppet of a mind
that rides eye high
in the sedan chair of its head
and steers it with its rods and strings
in jerky, awkward movement.

My mind is not a lonely recluse
staring out its eye windows
wishing it could move with grace
and interact, and know some body.

Nexus more than locus
in dynamic intersection
Nodes of pulsing energy
Swift connecting unity
No disembodied mind
No mindless body:
one being that is won
living in the One.

Body Rapture

Let the body rapture
lead you out
beyond the tentacles of words
beyond the weights and measures of the mind
The body knows it loves, it doesn't care
about constraints of boxes and conditions
doesn't need permission
doesn't need directions
has its own affection
makes its own connection
precisely tuned to every move and glance
The body rapture knows
love is pure enough to move you
in the deep perfection
of the dance.

Permission

You don't need permission
for you always have permission
to be you
You don't need to worry
for inside you know most surely
what is true
Each moment is a work of art
to which you bring your own true heart
Your heart will tell you truly what to do.

No need to be guessing
if your long-awaited blessing
will come through
Everything you're longing for
has always been here, and belonged
to you
Within the bud the flower grows
The time will come when it will show
Your garden blossoms plentiful and true.

So across your landscape
May you reap your understanding
Ever new
No need for pretending
for your heart will keep ascending
guiding you
to everything you're meant to be,
to do the work that sets you free
and shines you forth as royal, pure, and true.

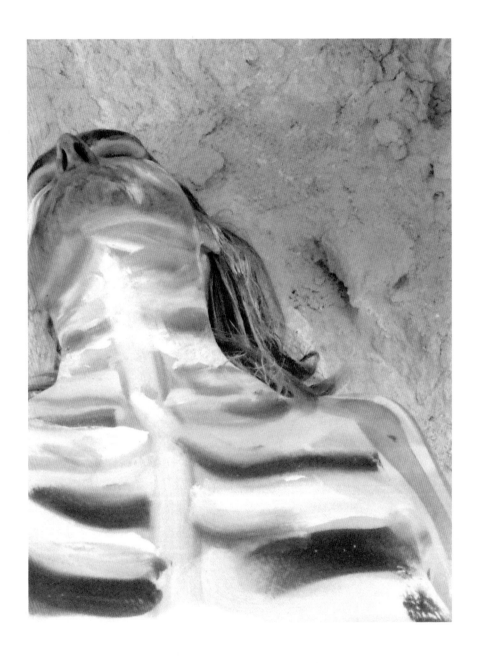

Work in Progress

Today the tasks
were taupe and black
The day was gray and green
My hobbled thought kept limping back
to what it all must mean
Let go, let go
It isn't here
The things that cease to matter
though mounded high
will disappear
in so much empty clatter
Last night my sleep was sweet and rich
My dreams were entertaining
though when I woke
they all dispersed
without a trace remaining
Today some friends were tired and sad
in pain or in despair
I reached to them across the space
and grasped at empty air
I yearn, I yearn
to offer peace
Some day I'll learn to do it
To open up that hidden door
and walk on with them
through it.

End of day

end of day
wounds return from their adventures
thoughts grow quiet
lights go down
and my body
curls up inside myself
like a child
to be held
to be healed
to be whole
in the deep trust of sleep
sure that Mind
will re-image every cell
realign every thought
knit all broken parts together
and come morning
shine my being through me once again.

In the Valley of Bones
(Ezekiel 37)

in the history of each half-lived life
so many bones
so many broken things
abandoned promises, buried dreams
sunken hopes with all their limp and dangling tendrils

(this is what I was going to be
this is what I meant to create
this was the early childhood promise
that was blighted by some careless, heavy hand)

fear not
each of these gets to rise
each one gets to join with others
as was intended, as was designed
to form a perfect arc
through which can pulse
the light of life
illumine everything
redeem each fallen chance

son of man, can these bones live?
can the mighty wind of oneness
unite their spirit again?
look
look and see
even the rise of that
one small tendril
is your proof.

Your spirit wins

When there is no way to win
and your spirit throws itself down
one or more of many thwarted paths
the failure says, you're wrong
your choice is bad
your blighted life
is all your fault
though you may flail
and cry out, crazed, for justice,
the censure drowns your voice.

When there is no way to win
in this world
your spirit still forges itself
a rare and brilliant thing
unseen by all the dust its rays illumine
unnoticed in the thrust of day's relentless gloom
till love's ablutions wash it clean
and there it shines
a light that overcomes the world.

Epiphany

You don't have to wait for joy
It's not contingent
on conditions
things you need to do to earn it
strings of power others hold,
gurus, teachers, texts to learn it
being not too young or old

You don't have to wait for joy
It doesn't hinge
on times and tasks that need to come together
or alignment of the stars and weather
It's here
Sure as you are

Illusion's claims will never
of their own accord
let you off the hook
They'll always book another thing
you have to wait for first
But you don't have to wait for joy
Here:
It's here
Sure as you're alive
Close as your daily breath.

Receiving

I won't dismiss as ego
The need to be received
Wrapped in a soft receiving blanket
Passed from arm to arm, enchanting
Cooed over
Welcomed
And cradled then especially
in loving and protective arms
To look out knowing
You are guarded fiercely
and treasured more than anything before.

Why should we think this need would go away
because our bones have grown
our circles widened out?
This need must grow apace with all our being
To knit us to our tribe
and show us how
in turn, we're made to so receive each other
To welcome, to accept, respect and love
An ancient need that we must now recover
to reach our peace, our purpose, and our home.

Your Purity

Your purity is not achieved
through negatives —
through not doing
not thinking
not feeling

Your purity, like that of mountain streams
is won by jumping forth
Leaping in the love of life
Taking on everything
Clearing the stream bed
through unrepressed movement
Hurtling free
with the forces that gather
Learning your essence
by being.

You might want to know

In the end
it doesn't matter
who you thought you were
or why you thought you couldn't —
Your light outshines the shapes you made
for it to show through
You dazzle us
which meets your deep design
not engineered by recoil or by intellect
but by an essence
eons older than you think you are
So there
You've done it
and the echoes of our shared delight
reverberate in bliss
so now you know
you didn't need to worry
This is who you've always been
This is who you are.

Emptiness

Only things that can receive
can be empty.
Consider this, O hearts, O arms —
The grand capacity of your design
How expertly you have been made
To hold, to take in
shelter and contain
To heal, embrace,
and then release again
To empty, fill, and so engage
in life, the grand enacting of creation
Exultant in its endless generation.

Soul Retrieval

No, no,
This is not the promise you were given
Mountains of detritus,
Self-enforced confinement
Stress and tracks of weary years
across your face

No
This is not your course
The clock-enforced conformity
The envious and jealous stabs within
Reflexive judgement,
Passing down the curse
of being conquered

However much the rules you're taught
claim to control
You never could be severed
from your soul

Hold with me now
Together, let's sing your song
It leads you back along the lines of longing
Where you have always sensed that you belong
We'll all converge there jubilantly thronging
At home as if we never had been gone
Let our eyes now feed each others embers
Resurrect our light so we remember
What had seemed so lost from us, so far
Who we've ever been
And who we are.

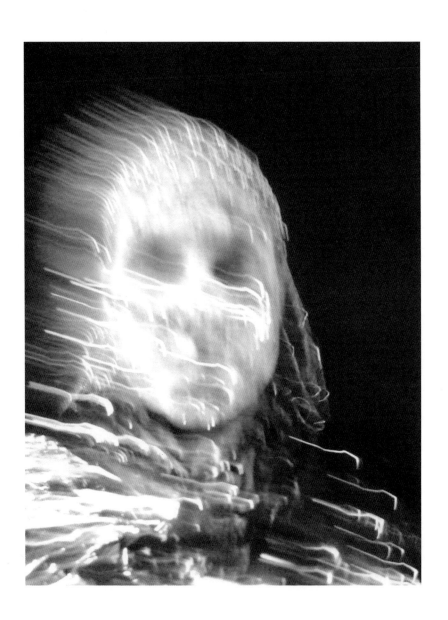

The worth of a life

What is the worth of a life?
Is there a metric for this?
Consider the sun on the water
The sparkling path
which always presents itself
right where you are:
Each sparkle is for you—
the meeting of light with your eyes—
Though others will see sparkles too,
they aren't the same ones that you view.

What is the worth of a life?
As if you could separate
one life from all others—
From the sun's sparkles, isolate one
Take it away from the sun . . .
What is the worth of a life?
There is no measure for this
No way the question can make any sense
It's worth everything that there is.

For you

What's needed here will not be said with words
though if I knew the magic words, I'd use them
And I don't need to understand the whys
the rationale, the story - not that I'd refuse them
Just that somewhere deep beneath the story
a universal need peeks through, quite clear
To feel the arms that always reach out for you
the endless depth to which you are held dear
Though these are just my arms, I hope they show you
(as any person's arms perhaps could do)
What joy it gives the Infinite to know you
How precious is your essence, and how true
No sentencing can stand, however tough
You walk in grace, and grace is good enough.

The need to be witnessed

It is not too much to ask
to have someone to take
by the hand
To lead down corridors
of memory, experience, imagination
To say to: look—here's a picture of me
as a child
And here's the song that still reminds me
of that summer back in '78
full of sun and angst and wild escape
And here's a thing I learned in Italy
along the streets of Florence

It's not too much to ask
to have someone who keeps
a special box for treasures
tucked in an honored place
inside their mind
to put the things you share
and take them out
and look at them sometimes

And yes, you'll keep a treasured box
for all the things your friend has shared
You'll take them out in gratitude
You'll love them, since you care

No need to strive for some
prescribed degree of fitness
It's not too much to ask
to have a witness.

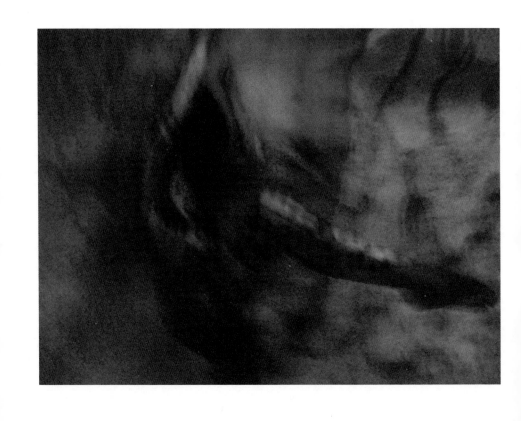

Weight and Lightness

Nothing in this world —
Nothing —
Not houses, not credentials
Not webs of friendship —
Has any strength to hold
the steady falling of the heart
They break like spider silk
against its weight
And it will fall right through
until it feels
the centered force of its own gravity
Until it slows
in thoughtful drift
and feels the atmosphere that gathers
meditatively
around its presence

Everything in this world —
Everything —
Each sense of home, each memory
Each smile exchanged —
Has grace to hold
the precious light that shines upon it
Grace to catch that light
and shine it forth
and be illuminated
Light that has no weight
That sits so brightly
on each snow crystal, each
hair of thistle down, each poised hope
that meekly lifts itself
into its own being.

Equilibrium

Let your peace return,
spiral inward, homing
There is no perturbation
that can mar its coming

In your internal quiet
the steady pulsing
has never ceased
This reassertion of itself
it does with ease

Outside, the winds may buffet you
May tease along your furls
Try to unravel you
Surge, hiss, seethe
Set you flapping, fraying
Worry at the edges of your poise

But underneath
The currents run their course
untouched by surface winds
And the soft voice
that's anchored in the truth
of who you are
Will spread its deep, pervasive calm
in strong and tranquil rays
across your sphere.

More

I am eager
even impatient
Is it appropriate
that one so seasoned
as years would peg me
should want so much
keep wanting more
to find the sip, instead of satiating
rouses thirst from deep within my core?
It doesn't matter
I will not be staid
I can't suppress myself
I will not be downplayed
I run each day
to scan for germination
peeking green between the clods
I know it doesn't work to pull the seeds up
but I urge them, nudge them with my thoughts
I'll call it revolution
in which we're all involved
I'll seek a steady motion
that need not be resolved
I'll polish my intention
and keep on planting seeds
till the harvest is sufficient
to satisfy these needs.

All I want

All I want
is everything —
It's not too much to ask
All I want is oneness
To soar in tune
in the surging seething symphony
of being
To be the roaring pounding flow
of all things living
To have my own song
constantly meet its harmony
My rhythm locked ecstatically
in polyrhythmic counterpoint
My down-bounce catapulting
someone else's flight
All I want
in this moment
is the bright contact
that multiplies light
That pulses back the richest chord
and wraps us
in its sacred ring of sound.

Time In

Let me give you a "time in" —
A time of contact,
of enough cuddle
to be an answer to your lost cries

A time in
Like time before time
when everyone knew
what to do about cries
that cry meant cuddle me
Bring me in
Let me know home

Oh yes
Now is the time
for time in
for everyone:
The hothead
The curmudgeon
The one who cringes inside his shell
darting in alarm at each approach
The one who sits alone
The one who sits with all her so-called friends
hiding isolation under loud words
The ones who make their dogged resolutions
with no idea what would earn the "in" ticket
The ones who hide their keening under sharp motion
The ones who try all day but can't fix it

Oh World!
Let us give each other time in
Let us come home into connection
until we have the circuits to unite
in tender understanding and affection.

Metamorphosis

Nothing stops the peace
of this release:
The shrunken husk,
the burst cocoon,
curls in upon itself
and so recedes
No need to seek its cloister
anymore

The bright wings pumping full of life
stretching out to own a greater sphere
affirm my purpose
and epitomize
why I'm here

So I begin to learn
to move, inhabit this expansive dome
To seek the currents in the air
To find myself at home

And if I need to feel a close embrace
I'll seek it in a way that lets my wings stay free
Angelic cradling and seeing, face to face
how we embody what we're meant to be.

All I have

All I have
to give this love with
are my hands
My hands and my spirit
and my strong desire
How could I have thought
to leave them out
to give love telekinetically?
How was I not taught
to use everything I have
all of my consciousness
including my body
to tune and give this love?
Generations of us
grew up lost
but here it is:
my hands, my arms, my heart
all I have —
Now I am learning to use,
to give and receive this love,
all that I have
all that I am.

Song of the Eternal Body

Each of us is anciently wise
Each holds the source
of the essential sequences of being
Each integrally joined
to that one primal course
The pulse of life, its elemental meaning

Funny how the secret waits so silently
Day by day does nothing to assert itself
And yet, as oracle, will tell us when we ask
the things we thought were far beyond our grasp

Ripples of mirth, spreading of connection
Bands of support, in joyful integration
The poise of totally assured perfection
is celebrated here in exaltation

And it sings:
We are right here
Where music flows within
like breath, like blood
And light shoots through
like waves of impulse spreading
We are right here
We hold you timeless in the web of life
and everything comprising us is good.

Sun Catchers

These moments catch joy
as bubbles catch air and light
in the confluence
of attention and intention
Of expectation and surprise
Of readiness to be delighted
and whatever light refractor
floats into our sphere of interaction:

A bright, chance meeting in a crowded festival,
A long-awaited reuniting of the clan,
A perfect day, and freedom to ride into it
open, ready to be wafted to adventure,
Or this: a tent of time —
Enough of it together
for each of us to open up a secret treasure
to relish as we share it with each other

These lights may now be kept
trapped in the amber of memory
Where they can serve as talisman
against the darkness of tomorrow's doubts
Remind us, from our cloister,
How we can go out
like bubbles in the wind
and catch the light.

Witnessing Joy

I will be a witness for joy
however unsophisticated and ungainly
it may seem,
however unrefined

I will witness joy
against the voices that deny it,
those who say
you can't have joy unless you are naive;
your joy betrays
that you're a little blind

But I will be a witness for joy
For if it's present here
it's also possible
in other places

I will claim the simple joy of company
And I will claim the simple joy of music
And I will claim the simple joy of walking free
barefoot in grass, and the infusion
of a little bit of sun into the day

And I will notice:
Joy is held secure in Spirit —
ever present substance,
cause of Life's self-affirmation —
Every living thing can feel it, hear it
Life takes joy and rises up
unceasing in ebullient celebration.

I'm in

(Notes from the third seasonal five women gathering on Vashon)

We have inhabited
a place of waves
an ebb and flow of stories
diverse perspectives that we try to reconcile
the tossing circles constantly recurring
hope baubles bobbing on their glossy surface

They bob against the undertow of sadness
and the mind's attempt
to close the loop, to claim
the promised satisfaction dearly longed for
We can choose to float there
or step free . . .

. . . Winds wander
Waves slap along the shore
Clouds display themselves across the sky
I step now from the land of metaphor
into the day
where sun sweetens
and geese parade their young before our eyes
Warm sand and stones smell like seaweed
by my resting face
Bright water licks my resting feet

- - - >

61

I lie here and consider
Where do I immerse myself?
How do I join in this grand wheeling of the sky?
How do I find grounding in this
aliveness so much greater than
my little "I"?

I'll take all of it
Whatever is given
Whatever way I can be used
to heal the stories, serve the greater vision
I'm ready
I'll take all immersions offered

I feel and smell the sun, the sand
the stones, the water
Then the waves come for me
and I'm in.

About the Artists

Wendy Mulhern is a poet, a dancer, a truth seeker. Her motto is *begin each day with prayer, end it with a poem; everything in between is dance.* Her prayer practice is longstanding; ecstatic dance is a much newer discovery, serving as a marvelous practicum for the spirituality her prayer calls forth. Poetry, while not a completely new expression for her, became a daily discipline in 2011. She has found that the three pursuits together complement one another and help her embody a greater truth. She still finds herself on the growing tip of discovery; still feels the daily excitement of it. She posts her daily poems in her blog, *Earth Whispering* (http://wendymulhernpoetry. blogspot.com/). For more information on her publications, see her website http://www.wendymulhern.com/.

Mellissae Lucia is an artist and adventurer, dancing and dreaming for the earth. She has published a limited edition book of her *Earthen Bod* photographic series, and created the visionary *Oracle of Initiation* divination deck with the accompanying book *Oracle of Initiation: Rainbows in the Dark.* In 2012 she was the subject of a documentary film called *Painted in the Desert*, produced by MK Barr, covering her journeys into the wilds of New Mexico. www.OracleofInitiation.com; www. PaintedintheDesert.com. The images in *Infinite Permission* are unretouched photographs taken by the artist, featuring herself and also Trevahr Hughes, Margi Halfon, Coleen Renee, and Lyric Kali.